Office Talk

Working in an English-Speaking Office

Myeong-Hee Seong
Casey Freeman

BAEKSAN Publishing Co

TABLE OF CONTENTS

Unit 1

The Job Interview

Introductions, handshakes and answering questions

Unit 1

The Job Interview

Introductions, handshakes and answering questions

Themes and Topics for This Chapter

Introductions

Handshake or a Bow?

Documents

Experience

Dress to Impress

Answering and Asking Questions

This Lesson's Vocabulary

Handshake	Documents	Experience	Prepare
Land	Interview	Interviewer	Interviewee
Dead Fish	Finger Breaker	Mission Statement	Influence
Presence	Potential	Web	Pump

TOPIC

How to Interview for a Job in an English-Speaking Office

Congratulations! You've landed a job interview for an English-speaking company. Unfortunately, interviewing for a job can be incredibly stressful for anybody, but this is a required skill you must learn if you want to work for an English-speaking company. The best bet with job interviews is to be prepared!

First, you should research the company you want to work for. This may seem obvious, but sometimes a job seeker will interview, but know nothing about the job or the company. This is not the first impression you want to give! Find out as much information as you can about their history, products, mission statement and business practices. You should write down notes about what you find to be important or interesting.

Next, consider questions your interviewer will ask you. There will be some personal questions about where you are from, your school and hobbies. What experience do you have in our field? Why do you want to work for our company? How can your presence influence our company? What would you like to change, contribute, edit or improve? Sometimes your interviewer may even ask, "How long would you like to work for us?" Another good idea is to prepare questions you would like to ask the interviewer. You can ask about the hours, any projects you would be assigned to, benefits package, how many people have interviewed for the position and the very important question: "How should I contact you to find out about the position?" Generally, Americans and Europeans save questions about the amount of salary or bonuses for the end of the interview.

Now is time to consider what to wear for an interview. Generally, the advice is to dress to impress. Both sexes should be well-groomed. Do not wear too much makeup, cologne or perfume. Men will wear a brown, black, blue or gray suit with a solid-colored or white shirt. The tie should be conservative. Most men in western countries do not wear the "shiny" suits that some Koreans prefer. Women can wear a suit or other respectable business attire such as a long skirt or a pants outfit. This is a job interview, not a date, so do not dress to look sexy. Either high heels or flat shoes are both acceptable. Women can wear brighter colors than men.

When the interview date comes, be sure to know how to get to the location and how long the transit will take. Showing up late to an interview is a sure way not to receive the desired position. Most people advise interviewees to arrive about 15 to 30 minutes early. As you wait, look over your résumé, your question list or the documents you brought. Don't play video games, text message or chat on your phone. In fact, make sure your phone is off and away. You do not want to be distracted.

When somebody calls your name, now begins one of the most important introduction events: the handshake. You may ask your interviewer how they would like to be addressed. They may just tell you using their first name is acceptable. Most interviewers will appreciate seeing a smile from the interviewee. This helps to show you are not nervous. You will be offered a chair, so maintain good posture. Do your best not to "um," "uh" or mumble during your speaking. Since you are not a native speaker, do your best to use English clearly and slowly to avoid any confusion. If the interviewer talks too fast, you may request a slower speed. As for yourself, talk at a medium pace. People who talk too slowly are sometimes perceived as less intelligent, but people who blurt their words out too quickly are thought to be nervous.

Most interviews last between five to thirty minutes. As the interview comes to a close, the interviewer may ask you if you have any questions. This is when your earlier prepared questions will come in handy. At the end, stand up, and if you have one, hand your business card to your interviewer. If they take it one handed, place it on their desk instead of their pocket or fold it, do not be offended. Business cards are not as important in the Western world as in Korean or Asian cultures. You may ask for theirs and take it according to your usual custom.

As you leave, you can ask "When should I expect to hear about the results of this interview?" Also say, "Thank you for your time and meeting with me today." As soon as you can, write an e-mail to the interviewer thanking them for the opportunity to interview and that you are interested in the job. This will keep you in the interviewer's mind and is always a nice gesture. You may need to interview for multiple different jobs, but with a little luck and persistence, you should be employed in no time!

READING COMPREHENSION

1. Review this list of vocabulary words and then translate the words into Korean.

ENGLISH	KOREAN	ENGLISH	KOREAN
Handshake		Experience	
Land		Presence	
Documents		Mission Statement	
Interview		Web	
Interviewer		Prepare	
Interviewee		Potential	
Gesture		Influence	
Perceived		Position	

2. Match the following synonyms with vocabulary words from Question 1.

a. Plan ______________________

b. Sway ______________________

c. Acquire ______________________

d. Papers ______________________

e. Conference ______________________

3. Read the statements. Can you tell if they are true or false?

a. Women should dress as sexy as possible for a job interview. T/F

b. Westerners treat business cards differently than Koreans. T/F

c. You should write possible questions when preparing for an interview. T/F

d. A handshake is not important. T/F

e. If your interviewer has a copy of your résumé, you do not need to give it to them again. T/F

f. Asking about the salary or benefits of a job is acceptable. T/F

g. Most job interviews last about ten minutes. T/F

h. Sending a thank you e-mail is considered a rude gesture. T/F

WORK WRITING

Now it's time to write five of your own questions that you would ask if somebody was interviewing for a job at your company. Would you ask about their university? Their past work experience? How they came to this country if they are a foreigner? Their church? Their hobbies? Be creative!

ROLE PLAY

Practice this conversation with at least one other friend.

John Smith: Interviewer

Mary Adams: Interviewee

John: Miss Adams, I will see you now.

Mary: (Stand up) I am Mary Adams. Nice to meet you. (Shake hands)

John: How are you today?

Mary: I'm very excited to interview with you today.

John: Great news. Come into my office and sit down.

Mary: Thank you.

John: So why would you like to work with our company?

Mary: I believe that you are a leader in your field, and with my experience, skills and work ethic, I believe I can become a great addition as well as contributing employee for your company.

John: Good answer. Do you have any questions for me?

Mary: Yes, actually. What are the salary and benefits of this position?

John: We offer a competitive salary and a full benefits package. That is all for our interview, you may leave now.

Mary: Thank you for your time and consideration. (Shake hands again.) When can I expect to hear the results of the interview?

John: We will contact you.

Mary: Thank you. Goodbye.

LET'S DISCUSS

Speak with other students about job interviews.

1. How should you look for information about a company for a job interview?

a. Where will you find information about the company?

b. What information is most important?

c. How will you present this information to your interviewer?

2. How should you dress for a job interview?

a. What should men wear?

b. What should women wear?

c. What are the differences between acceptable Korean clothes and Western clothes?

3. How can you prepare to predict as well as answer questions the interviewer will ask you?

a. How would you talk about your past experience?

b. How can you discuss your university education?

c. How can coming from Korea be a benefit?

4. What types of questions can you ask your interviewer?

a. What interests you most about a job?

b. Should you ask about the salary, hours or requirements? Why or why not?

c. How are these questions different than in Korea?

5. How do Koreans in business situations greet each other?

a. What can you tell about somebody from the way they shake a hand or bow?

b. What do you dislike about shaking a person's hand?

c. How can you practice shaking a hand?

MORE DISCUSSION

1. **Discuss with a partner, what types of questions would you ask if you were interviewing for these types of jobs?**

Manager at a Restaurant	
Pilot	
Delivery Driver	
Advertising Representative	
Korean Language Teacher at a University	
Coffee Shop Barista	
Account Manager	
Dental Assistant	

2. **What would you wear to a job interview? On your head? Around your neck? What type of shirt? What style and color of suit? What type of shirt? If you are a woman, what type of pants or skirt? What kind of shoes? Would you use a perfume or cologne?**

SOME THINGS TO REMEMBER

How to Shake a Hand

1. A handshake is the way people are greeted in western society, and often people are judged by this. A proper handshake is when the area on your right hand between your thumb and index finger – or web – touches the web of the other person.

2. A medium amount of pressure is applied by all fingers and thumb. You don't want to be a "dead fish" (a limp handshake) or a "finger breaker" (too strong).

3. Only one up-and-down motion – a pump – is necessary. After the pump, release. As you become familiar with a person, you may put your left hand on the other person's hand or shoulder, but do not do this upon a first meeting.

4. If you are accustomed to bowing, you may do so during the handshake, but this is not required.

More Tips for Job Interviews

1. At the beginning of the interview, you should give a copy of your résumé to the interviewer. They may already have it, but having a résumé handy is a good sign that you are prepared. If you want to show the interviewer about your past projects from school or work, give your interviewer a printed example – if you have them.

2. Make sure you have everything you need. You should bring a binder, folder or document case with you. Include at least three copies of your résumé, cover letter, list of references, letters of recommendation, driver's license or identification card and any reports, surveys, presentations or projects that can print out and hand to your potential employer.

Unit 2

Those Annoying Pieces of Paper

Making a stellar résumé

Unit 2

Those Annoying Pieces of Paper

Making a stellar résumé

Themes and Topics for This Chapter

Reasons for a résumé

Résumé Rules

Making yourself stand out

Objective

Background

This Lesson's Vocabulary

Résumé	Objective	Truth	White Lie
Fluency	Grammar	Spellchecker	Background
Flattering	Action verbs	Sum Up	Applicant
Relevant skills	Barred	Margins	Font

TOPIC

Writing a Top Notch Résumé

Tell me everything about yourself, but only on one sheet of paper. Yikes! How can you sum up your entire life and experiences on just a single page of A4 paper? Well, it seems nobody likes writing them, but unfortunately, displaying your high points in your résumé is one of the most important steps in looking for a job.

Interviewers use résumés to check potential employees' backgrounds and to see if the applicant possesses the skills necessary to perform the duties the job requires. An interviewer will look at your work experience, your school history, relevant skills, volunteer efforts and even hobbies to see if you are a right fit for a job.

Generally, your résumé should be about one to two pages long. Most American companies require your résumé to be only a single page. You can adjust size of the margins, fonts, spacing and indents to include more information, but do not make the mistake of putting too much on your résumé or making the letters too small, because then it will be too hard for your interviewer to read.

Job seekers usually use Microsoft Word to write their documents. If you have a similar document-writing program on your computer that is acceptable, but make sure you save it in the format the interviewer requires. Some may accept HTML, PDF or ASCII. Double check to ensure you submit your résumé correctly. A handwritten résumé is never allowed in a professional environment.

At the top should be your name, address and contact information such as your cell phone number and e-mail address. After that is when writing a résumé can become tricky and annoying, because so many different styles and opinions differ on what to put on next. You can include your Work Objective. If this is your first job, you may include your education, including dates you attended your university, your major, specialized classes you took and your grade point average (GPA). If you already have work experience, you will want to tell which company you worked for, what your job responsibilities were, how long you worked there and if you were promoted, received awards or any changes you made to the company's policies, products or management style.

Towards the end you may talk about relevant skills you possess. For example, if you will be working with computers at your job, explain how you fixed computers or know how to use certain programs related to the job you are applying for. Also near the bottom of your résumé, if you have them, include your volunteer activities, such as teaching orphans, church activities or anything you did out of the kindness of your heart and were not paid for. You may include clubs you belong to, hobbies or interests. The information at the bottom will be the least important, and can be cut out of your résumé if you are running out of space. At the very end, you should include the line "References: Given Upon Request." Usually, you will include list of references anyway, but adding this line looks professional and shows that people are willing to speak about you on their behalf.

When you write a résumé, you need to make yourself sound as flattering as possible, without lying. Many studies show that almost half of the résumés out there contain many falsifications about the résumé writer. While lying on your résumé may earn you the job, what happens when you are not able to live up to your résumé? You may be fired, or worse yet, barred from working in your field ever again! So that little white lie you tell may not be worth the risk in the long run. However, your résumé should only contain positive aspects about you and your experiences. Do not include anything negative about yourself such as if you are overweight, were fired from a job or constantly arrive late. This is a sure way not to be hired.

Using a spellchecker or grammar checker will help you find misspelled words or other mistakes, but will not find everything. A good suggestion is to ask an English-speaking friend or teacher to look through your résumé to try and correct errors.

You don't want your interviewer to be the one who discovers your blunders!

Your résumé should only give information about your experiences, skills, history and your work objectives. Your cover letter will allow you to show more of your personality, but that's another story, and another chapter...

Here is a very good sample résumé for somebody applying to be a dental assistant.

Andy Quickenstein
21 West Jump Street,
Carlisle, CA 01741
(123) 456-7890
aquickie@gmail.com

Objective Seeking a challenging position to work as a Dental Assistant.

Work Experience:

- 2003-present Michael Davis, DDS California, CAX-Ray and Dental Assistant
- 2003-present George Stevenson, DDS California, CAX-Ray and Dental Assistant
- 2002-2003 Jenny Hofstra, D.M.D./C Belmont, D.M.D. Endodontist California, CAX-Ray and Dental Assistant
- 1995-2002 Molly Major, DDS California, CAX-Ray and Dental Assistant

Education:

1998-2002, ABC College Belmont, California, GPA 3.6
Major: Dental Hygienic Science
*Took multiple classes on Dental Hygiene and Teeth Whitening Technology.
*Studied under world famous dental practitioner Betsy Marmalade.
*Graduated at the top of the class and received Dean's List Awards.
C.P.R. Certified
OSHA Certified

Skills:

- Took and mixed impressions; disinfected and operated autoclave.
- Four-handed chair-side; take developed and mount x-rays.
- Trimmed models, made trays/temps and OSHA-prescribed sterilizations.
- Operated the ultra-sonic post-operative instruction and oral hygiene as well as period charting.
- Handled front desk operations.

Hobbies:

- California Marathoners' Club: I run a marathon almost every month and help organize meetings.
- Hip Dips Turtle Rescue: On weekends I assist in the conservation of sea turtle habitat.

Reference:

Available upon request.

READING COMPREHENSION

1. Review this list of vocabulary words and then translate the words into Korean.

ENGLISH	KOREAN	ENGLISH	KOREAN
Résumé		Truth	
Fluency		Spellchecker	
Flattering		Sum up	
Relevant skills		Margins	
Objective		White Lie	
Grammar		Background	
Action verbs		Applicant	
Barred		Font	

2. Use five of these words or phrases in sentences.

a. Sum up ______________________________

b. White lie ______________________________

c. Barred ______________________________

d. Truth ______________________________

e. Margins ______________________________

3. Read the statements. Can you tell if they are true or false?

a. A résumé can be any length you choose. T/F

b. The most important information should be at the bottom of a résumé. T/F

c. A résumé is how an interviewer determines if you are right for a position. T/F

d. You can choose not to include your hobbies or clubs in your résumé. T/F

e. Including humor in your résumé is a good idea. T/F

f. You never want to include negative aspects of your history in a résumé. T/F

g. You should not include your salary requirements in a résumé. T/F

h. Spell and grammar checking tools will find all your mistakes. T/F

4. Write your answers to the following questions.

a. What will you include at the top of your résumé?

____

b. Who can you ask to look over your résumé? Why would you choose that person?

____

c. How long will it take you to write a résumé?

____

WORK WRITING

Now it's time to write your own résumé. Look at the example on page 22, and insert your information over the samples. Be sure to have a friend or teacher proofread your work!

ROLE PLAY

Practice this conversation with at least one other friend.

Sue: Job Seeker

Bill: English Professor

Sue: Hello professor, I was wondering if you have time. Could you please look through my résumé to make sure I have no mistakes?

Bill: I would be happy to. Can you e-mail it to me?

Sue: Yes, I already did. I hope that is okay.

Bill: What format did you use?

Sue: I used the new version of Microsoft Word.

Bill: That's great. Everybody uses that.

Sue Well, what did you think?

Bill: Personally, I prefer to display your work experience on top, rather than your education. But if you like it that way, you may do it.

Sue: Did you find any errors?

Bill: Here under your education, it says you attended university from February 2011 to December 2008. Those dates appear to be wrong. What is the correct time?

Sue: Oh no! I meant to say I attended university from February 2008 until December 2011.

Bill: Well, that's an easy correction. Make sure you fix that before you send it to your interviewer.

Sue: Thank you so much for your help. Do you think it is long enough?

Bill: Usually, companies want only one-to-two pages, so I think your page-and-a-half will be fine. If you want to cut anything, I would get rid of your section about the clubs you belonged to in order to make the résumé only one page long.

Sue: Thank you.

LET'S DISCUSS

Speak with other students about writing a résumé.

1. What is most difficult about writing a résumé?

a. What do you prefer at the top? At the bottom?

b. Will you include your hobbies? Why?

c. How long do you want your résumé to be?

2. What are common mistakes on résumés?

a. How can you catch these mistakes?

b. Who would you ask to help you?

c. Why do interviewers request the same format or color of paper?

3. Why do you think having a perfect résumé is so important?

a. What can you do with your résumé to help you stand out?

b. Why do so many people lie on their résumés?

c. What types of problems could occur if your employer finds out you lied?

4. What do you think is more important, your work or your school experience?

a. Which of your school experiences is most impressive?

b. What will you say about you work experience?

c. If you have no work experience, what can you say instead?

5. If you apply for different types of jobs, would you write different résumés?

a. What type of résumé would you write for a management position? Optometrist assistant? Barista at a café?

b. Do you think your résumé is a good view of who you really are? Why?

c. Should people all write the exact same style of résumé? Why?

More Discussion

Discuss with a partner which of these clubs, hobbies or skills are acceptable to include in your résumé. Why or why not would you include them?

Swimming Team	
Management Intern	
Volunteering at Your Church	
Hamburger Lovers' Association	
Beer Drinkers Club	
Cheerleading	
Business Leaders' Club	
Teaching Old People to Use Cell Phones	

SOME THINGS TO REMEMBER

Seven More Tips When Writing a Résumé

There are many rules for résumés, but most of them are just guidelines.

1. A general rule of thumb is to be consistent. Use the same font and size throughout the entire résumé. If you capitalize or "bold" one of your headings, do it for all of them. Make sure your résumé looks organized and not "thrown together."

2. Write your résumé at least two different times, one with your education on top and one with your work experience on top. Which do you like better?

3. Putting your name a little bigger or in bold is a good idea to help grab the attention of your interviewer, but don't make your name too large. That looks like you are bragging or have nothing to say.

4. Make sure your e-mail address is appropriate. Do not include an e-mail addresses with words like "cool guy@gmail.com," "prettyprincess@hotmail.com" or "superbeerdrinker@yahoo.com." You may want to set up a new professional e-mail address. Many people use Gmail and it is a free service.

5. Try to keep your bullet points and other information orderly and in a straight line.

6. Print out many copies of your résumé. You will need them for job interviews and you never know when you will meet somebody who can pass them on!

7. Almost everybody suggests that your résumé be printed on white paper. While it is important to stand out of the crowd, in some cases this may be a bad thing. Many companies instantly discard résumés printed on colored paper.

Unit 3

Those Annoying Pieces of Paper

Making a stellar cover letter

OFFICE TALK

Working in an English-Speaking Office

Unit 3

Those Annoying Pieces of Paper

Making a stellar cover letter

Themes and Topics for This Chapter

Creativity

Writing Skills

Discussing Experience

Diversity

Personalizing

This Lesson's Vocabulary

Plain	Shine	Unique	Highlight
Tailor-made	Skeleton	Copy and paste	Prospective
Title	Diverse	Encourage	Overseeing
Mutually	Convenient	Proofread	Personality

TOPIC

Writing a Top Notch Cover Letter

Résumés and cover letters are usually best friends. When you apply to a job, employers will want to see both. However, while very similar, they are also very different. Today we will talk about cover letters.

First, as the name implies, the cover letter goes on "top" of your résumé – or "covers" it. Think of your cover letter as the cover to a book. You want the cover of your book to be exciting, interesting and attractive. All this builds up interest in what is inside the cover – your résumé! While a résumé is usually a very plain sheet full of your professional and educational information, a cover letter lets your writing skills and personality shine. This isn't to say writing cover letters is easier, in some ways, it can be more difficult. While you may send the same exact résumé to just about every job posting (with a few changes here and there), each cover letter you write must be unique for the job you are applying to. A cover letter is generally less than one page.

Along with being tailor-made for each position, your cover letter needs to do more than just cover your résumé. You need to explain who you are, why you are sending a résumé, why the person should read your résumé, how you learned about the position or the business, highlight important pieces of your background, inform about your availability, as well as show your attitude and personality.

Most cover letters follow the same format: your name and address, the company's name and address and then a greeting using the prospective interviewer's name or title. Now for the first paragraph, you will state why you are writing this cover letter, what position you are interested in, how you learned about the company or the job, and a little basic information about yourself. Again, this may sound a lot more difficult than it has to be. Here's a simple example:

Dear Mr. Smith,

My name is Hank Dean and I am very interested in the management job you listed on the Venture Company website. I am a recent graduate of State University, where I majored in management techniques. With my education and diverse background, I believe I could bring many qualities to your company.

In the second paragraph you will explain why you are interested in the employer, the job or the type of job. Remember: tell them not only that you are interested, but WHY you are interested. This paragraph is where you will explain more about your school or past work experience. This is also a chance to encourage the reader to look for your résumé.

I learned about Venture in my university and studied all about the company, the products and its history. For the past three years, I worked as a manager at Isis Financial Group, overseeing international projects and the development of new products. This experience readied me for work with the Venture Company in many other ways. I ask that you see my enclosed résumé for more information.

For your final paragraph, indicate that you would like to interview for the position or talk with the employer to learn more about the job or their plans to hire people. Tell them a few convenient days or times you can meet.

I think your groundbreaking company and my rapidly rising career are a perfect match for each other. This month, I would like to schedule a mutually convenient time for us to meet.

At the end, be sure to thank the reader and leave space above your name for your signature, even if you are not going to sign the cover letter yourself. You may mail the cover letter in an envelope, or e-mail it using the same program you used to write your résumé.

Go through the cover letter carefully to find any misspellings or other errors. Again, ask a teacher or friend to help you. If you are going to use the same cover letter, then fill it in with copy and paste, and make sure you copy and paste the correct information! It's quite embarrassing to find out you sent the wrong addressed cover letter to a potential employee!

Here is an example of a cover letter

1000 Monarch Apts.
Bismarck, ND 26760
(123) 555-6789
bsampson@email.com

January 25, 2012

Ms. Natalie Johnson
Personnel Director
Venture Company
3507 Rusty St
Atlanta, GA 34395

Dear Ms. Johnson:

I read in the January 24th *Venture Company News* classified section of your need for a manager for one of your Washington, DC, area sites. I will be finishing university soon, and I believe that I have the necessary credentials for the project.

Every summer for the last five years I worked in my father's grocery store, starting as a basic cleaner and now manage the store when he is away on business. As indicated on my enclosed résumé, last summer I served as an assistant construction manager on a two million dollar residential construction project.

In addition to this practical experience, I will complete requirements for my B.S. in Management Practices from State University in May. As you may know, my university is one of the few universities in the country that offers such a specialized degree for the management industry. I am confident that my degree, along with my years of experience, make me an excellent candidate for your job.

The Venture Company projects are familiar to me, and my aspiration is to work for a company that has your excellent reputation. I would welcome the opportunity to interview with you. I will be available any time during the week. In the next week to ten days I will contact you to answer any questions you may have.

Thank you for your consideration.

Sincerely,
(handwritten signature)
Brock Simpson

Enclosure

READING COMPREHENSION

1. Review this list of vocabulary words and then translate the words into Korean.

ENGLISH	KOREAN	ENGLISH	KOREAN
Plain		Unique	
Tailor-made		Copy and paste	
Title		Encourage	
Mutually		Proofread	
Shine		Highlight	
Skeleton		Prospective	
Diverse		Overseeing	
Convenient		Personality	

2. Use five of the above words or phrases in sentences.

a. Tailor-made ______________________________

b. Mutually ______________________________

c. Proofread ______________________________

d. Highlight ______________________________

e. Personality ______________________________

3. Read the statements. Can you tell if they are true or false?

a. A cover letter goes on top of your résumé. T/F

b. Always personalize your cover letter for each job. T/F

c. A cover letter should never show your personality. T/F

d. A cover letter can be as long as you like it to be. T/F

e. You may cut and paste your cover letter. T/F

f. Cover letters explain the job. T/F

g. In the last paragraph, you state why you are writing this cover letter. T/F

h. You should find a native speaker to edit your cover letter. T/F

WORK WRITING

Now it's time to write your own cover letter. Again, you can look at the example, and insert your information over the samples. Be sure to have a friend or teacher proofread your work!

ROLE PLAY

Practice this conversation with at least one other friend.

Travis : Friend writing a cover letter

Becky : Friend proofreading a cover letter

Travis: Hey, buddy, can you help me look at my cover letter?

Becky: Of course! How can I assist you?

Travis: I'm not really sure this is what they want.

Becky: Well, let me read it first.

Travis: Does it look clear enough?

Becky: As I learned, when writing a cover letter, you need to show why you are writing, why you are interested in the job and then that you would like to meet.

Travis: Do you see anything I should change?

Becky: You should re-write your second paragraph.

Travis: How can I do that?

Becky: Instead of saying you "had a super good time" you should say you "learned much about the education field and learned a diverse set of skills."

Travis: Alright, well, I will look it over and I will fix the things that need fixing.

Becky: Good luck!

LET'S DISCUSS

Speak with other students about cover letters.

1. What do you think is more stressful, writing a cover letter or résumé? Why?

a. How can a cover letter be easier than a résumé? How can it be harder?

b. What might the most difficult part be about writing a cover letter?

c. Who can help you write a cover letter?

2. How can you best highlight your skills in your cover letter?

a. Will you use copy and paste in your cover letter? Why or why not?

b. How will you show your personality and interest in the job with your cover letter?

c. What are some common mistakes on cover letters?

3. Why do you think job seekers want to see your personality as well as experience?

a. What is a good personality to have in a work environment?

b. How can you write about your personality so that you can gain interest from companies?

c. What is more important, experience or personality?

4. Where can you find good examples of cover letters?

a. Does your country have something similar to a cover letter? If so, what?

b. What do you think is better, mailing or e-mailing?

c. Have you ever written a cover letter? How was the experience?

5. If you apply for different types of jobs, would you write different cover letters?

a. What type of cover letter would you write for a management position? Optometrist assistant? Barista at a café?

b. Do you think a cover letter is a good view of who you really are? Why?

c. Should all people write the exact same style of cover letter? Why or why not?

MORE DISCUSSION

Discuss with a partner which of these topics are acceptable to include in your cover letter. Why or why not would you include them?

Your university major	
How tall you are	
Why you are interested in this job	
How you are perfect for the job	
Your GPA	
Your work experience	
All of your friends in the business	
A favorite sport or TV program	

SOME THINGS TO REMEMBER

Four More Hints for Writing a Cover Letter

That sounds like a lot, doesn't it!? Well, writing a cover letter doesn't have to be a gigantic pain.

1. What most people do is write a "Skeleton" cover letter – which is a basis of their cover letter with blank spots where vital information should go. Then cover letter writers will create or copy and paste the most relevant information into the blank spots.

2. Even though you won't sign your name at the end of your cover letter if you e-mail, still leave room to go for the intended signature. This is also in case you want to print it, or to show the habit and tradition.

3. Make sure you check and double-check to see all the names, dates and companies are correct. Many people cut and paste the wrong information in cover letters, then send them out!

4. A cover letter should be on the same size and color paper as your résumé. However, if you choose to use different sizes and fonts for your documents, that is perfectly fine.

Unit 4

Elevator Speeches

Selling Yourself to Your Employer

OFFICE TALK

Working in an English-Speaking Office

Unit 4

Elevator Speeches

Selling Yourself to Your Employer

Themes and Topics for This Chapter

Confidence

Talking About Yourself

Salesmanship

Finding High Points about Your Past and Current Work or School Experiences

Summarizing Yourself, Your Goals and Your Past

This Lesson's Vocabulary

Elevator speech	Confidence	Salesmanship	Idol
Impression	Exercise	Qualities	Networking
Off the top of your head	Client satisfaction rate	Spunky	Frontrunner
Timely fashion	Corporate ladder	Moving up	Canned conversation

TOPIC

What's An Elevator Speech?

Imagine you are in an office building by yourself. You step into an elevator, and the only person inside is the head of the company you dream of working for. This person is an idol in the business world. This is only a one-minute elevator ride, so you need to have something ready to say to this person. What do you say to make a great impression? Your future just might depend on what people call: An Elevator Speech.

This may sound like a silly dream, but it is an exercise used to teach job seekers how to summarize their personality, qualities and work experience. Elevator speeches are quick talks designed to give the maximum amount of information in a minimum amount of time. Often, while looking for a job, you will need to talk to different executives, managers, your employed friends and friends of friends. So, instead of coming up with a new elevator speech off the top of your head, sit down and think of a proper set of topics to speak about to a person you would like to work for.

The person you will give the elevator speech to is your "target." Think about delivering a great speech as a goal. You need to prepare for any goal you reach. Potential employers want to know your personal, educational and work history. So think of what you did in the past, what you are doing now and what you are going to do in the future.

You can talk to your family, teachers and friends in order to find out the high points of your career thus far. Have you moved up the corporate ladder in a timely fashion? Do you work well with people? Are you always on time? This will be the "Present" portion of your elevator speech. Now talk about what you did for your former jobs, school or volunteer work. What are some of the accomplishments or changes you made? Did you start at the bottom and move your way up to the position as manager? Did you revolutionize the way things were done?

Next, people will be impressed about what you have done, but mostly they want to know what you will do for their company. So inform them about what you plan to do for them. What are the company's strong points? How could the company improve? What can you do to help? Make sure your personality, experience and goals are included in your elevator speech. Using humor is a great way to break the ice and ensure your target remembers you.

At the end, make sure you exchange information with the person. Try to obtain your target's work address or e-mail address and send them a "Thank You" note. Sometimes a little courtesy is all it takes!

READING COMPREHENSION

1. Review this list of vocabulary words and then translate the words into Korean.

ENGLISH	KOREAN	ENGLISH	KOREAN
Elevator speech		Confidence	
Impression		Exercise	
Off the top of your head		Client satisfaction rate	
Timely fashion		Corporate ladder	
Salesmanship		Idol	
Qualities		Networking	
Spunky		Front-runner	
Moving up		Canned conversation	

2. Use five of these words or phrases in sentences.

a. Impression ______________________________

b. Off the top of your head ______________________________

c. Spunky ______________________________

d. Confidence ______________________________

e. Front-runner ______________________________

3. Read the statements. Can you tell if they are true or false?

a. An elevator speech should be longer than one minute. T/F

b. You should always give your business card to a business idol. T/F

c. Elevator speeches are quick talks designed to give the maximum amount of information in a minimum amount of time. T/F

d. Your target is somebody you don't want to hire you. T/F

e. You ask for your target's e-mail information. T/F

f. Your past work experience does not matter with elevator speeches. T/F

g. Physical contact is required during an elevator speech. T/F

h. You should not include your future ideas for the company in an elevator speech. T/F

4. Answer the following questions.

a. What is something important you've done in the past?

____

b. What are you doing now to better yourself and your work prospects?

____

c. How can you use your personal talents to help a company in the future?

____

WORK WRITING

Now it's time to write your own elevator speech. Make sure to include your past work experiences, what you are doing now and how you will help the company in the future. What type of introduction will you make? How will you end your speech?

ROLE PLAY

Practice this conversation with at least one other friend.

Andy : Job Seeker

Jenny : Business Owner

Andy: Hi, I usually don't do this, but my name is Andy and I would really like to speak to you about why I would be perfect for your company.

Jenny: Nice to meet you, Andy. I'm listening.

Andy: First, I am currently going to school. However, in the future, I would like to work in your field because I have studied and read about your products. I think you run a fine company, but I believe I can help you improve your company because of my past experiences.

Jenny: Tell me a little bit about yourself.

Andy: I am from Korea. I studied very hard. Even so, I learned how to make long-lasting friends and network, which I believe will assist your company in growing.

Jenny: And what type of job experiences do you have?

Andy: I haven't worked for a company that is your size, and currently I'm studying, but I worked as a personal trainer in my gym, which helped teach me about designing unique exercise programs for different people as well as keeping clients happy. I'm always on time and my client satisfaction rate is sky high.

Jenny: That's good to know if I need to work out. What can you think is the most important business issue at the current moment?

Andy: I think research and development of the next generation of gadgets and technology, as well as practical uses of such devices, will show which company is the frontrunner of the business world.

Jenny: You're quite the spunky young person. Do you have a business card?

Andy: Yes, I do. Here you go.

Jenny: Thank you. I'd like to look over your résumé and if I like what I see, I'll contact you.

Andy: Thank you. It was nice to meet you.

Jenny: Nice to meet you, too.

LET'S DISCUSS

Speak with other students about elevator speeches.

1. What type of information would you include in your elevator speech?

a. What will you include about your past?

b. Your current self and work situation?

c. What will you do in the future?

2. What do you think about the other person's information?

a. What would you highlight?

b. What would you delete?

c. With what information should they start their elevator speech?

3. What types of body language should you use during your elevator speech?

a. What should you do with your hands?

b. How much eye contact do you think is appropriate?

c. Should you make physical contact with that person?

4. Where could you find people to give you elevator speech to?

a. What type of people would be good to practice with?

b. Who could help you write your speech?

c. How many times should you practice?

5. How should you dress when you give an elevator speech?

a. What if you are underdressed and run into your business idol? Will you speak to them?

b. What will you do if your business idol refuses to speak with you?

c. What are exercises you can do to increase your confidence while giving an elevator speech?

MORE DISCUSSION

Discuss with a partner which of these topics are acceptable to include in your elevator speech. Why or why not would you include them?

Types of parties you like	
What your major is	
Goals	
Religion	
Your first job	
How you were fired	
Friends in the business	
You read an article about your idol	

SOME THINGS TO REMEMBER

More Tips about Elevator Speeches

1. Of course, it's absolutely necessary to be polite and short. This won't be a long conversation.

2. Also, the target of your speech may be too busy to listen to your elevator speech. Do your best to get your business card or contact information in their possession, bid them "Goodbye" and hope for the best.

3 You want to shoot for an elevator speech that is about one-minute long. Anything longer might sounds like you are bragging or even worse, you might sound boring. Any shorter than 60 seconds and you might look like you've got nothing to say!

4. Don't Memorize! When people memorize speeches, they can sound like robots. You don't want to bore your target, you want to wow them with your dynamic voice and personality. Think about it, if somebody is selling something to you, do you want to hear some "canned conversation" that sounds like it has been repeated a million times, or do you want to listen to somebody come up with interesting things to say.

5. The likelihood you will actually be in an elevator with your idol is very low, but the possibility that you will use your elevator speech with somebody interested in hiring you is really high. Often people ask, "What's your elevator speech?" Don't "Um" and "Uh." Make sure you've got one!

Unit 5

To Be or Not To Be?

What to wear or not wear, talk about or not talk about

Unit 5

To Be or Not To Be?

What to wear or not wear, talk about or not talk about

Themes and Topics for This Chapter

Cultural Differences

Dress for Success

Small Talk

Appropriate Discussion Topics

Personal Information

This Lesson's Vocabulary

Conservative	Liberal	Practices	Guidelines
Acceptable	Appropriate	Reputation	Flashy
Leeway	Carrying on	Sporting event	Sexual requests
Happenings	Handbook	Racy	Chat

TOPIC

To Be or Not To Be?

There are many differences between Eastern and Western business practices, but also there are differences between how you act, dress and talk in the office. Every office will have a dress code, and most will be different, but in this chapter we will go over some clothing and conversation guidelines to keep your job and reputation safe.

Many companies will require conservative dress such as suits and ties; while others are much more liberal and may allow t-shirts, sneakers or blue jeans. The thing to remember is to dress appropriately for your company. During your interview, you definitely will want to wear something conservative. As your time at the company goes on, you may dress more to your style, but generally, keep the flashy jewelry, perfume, cologne and brighter colors at home. You certainly may "test the waters" with what will be acceptable, but don't show up to work at a formal office in a bikini!

Just as the manner of dress changes from office to office, appropriate topics of discussion also varies. Most human resources departments will hold meetings to inform you of acceptable and unacceptable small talk topics. Following these rules is an easy way to know if you are within the boundaries of your work's appropriate topics of talking. Failure to abide by the rules can be grounds for termination – which means you can get fired for telling a racy joke!

As a rule, if you would not openly discuss a topic with your parents or grandparents, that topic may not be acceptable to discuss in an office. Since English is not your first language, you may be given some leeway, but try to pick up what the other workers say for small talk and stick with what makes you comfortable. Chances are, if a discussion makes you uncomfortable, it could make other workers uncomfortable as well. This rule applies to jokes as well. Using humor is a great way to build friendships and break the ice. However, when jokes become offensive, problems in the business world arise. You should not crack jokes that ridicule one of the sexes, a race, religion or country. Sexual jokes and talks are almost never acceptable, especially when the opposite sex is around the discussion. Sexual requests or conquests are never spoken about in polite offices.

When carrying on small talk around the office, many workers will discuss the results of a recent sporting event, a television program or happenings in the news. If conversations grow in depth, you may continue on with them, but remember, you are at work to work, not to chat. Most offices will have a handbook about their small talk policies, be sure you read this and understand it. You do not want to be fired for something as stupid as telling a racy joke or talking with your friends too much.

READING COMPREHENSION

1. Review this list of vocabulary words and then translate the words into Korean.

ENGLISH	KOREAN	ENGLISH	KOREAN
Conservative		Practices	
Acceptable		Reputation	
Leeway		Sporting event	
Happenings		Racy	
Liberal		Guidelines	
Appropriate		Flashy	
Carrying on		Sexual requests	
Handbook		Chat	

2. Match the following synonyms with vocabulary words from Question 1.

a. Talk ____________________

b. Manual ____________________

c. Easy Going ____________________

d. Gaudy ____________________

e. Rules ____________________

3. Read the statements. Can you tell if they are true or false?

a. You may dress however you like for any business. T/F

b. The human resources department will discuss appropriate dress and acceptable small talk topics. T/F

c. An employee may be fired over a joke. T/F

d. You should dress conservatively at first, and then test the waters to dress the way you like. T/F

e. Sexual humor is not preferred in a professional office. T/F

f. Anything you talk about with your grandparents can be acceptable small talk. T/F

g. All companies have the same dress code in Western offices. T/F

h. Talking about sports is not considered small talk. T/F

4. Answer the following questions

a. How would you dress on the first day of work at a new office?

____

b. What is a topic you and your friends like to talk about? Is it appropriate for work?

____

c. List some appropriate small talk topics people should use in the office.

____

WORK WRITING

Speaking in the office is often difficult task for non-native speakers. Free write for 10 minutes about small talk. What are subjects you will talk about in your office? Are any of the rules in this book different than the Korean rules you are used to?

ROLE PLAY

Practice this conversation with at least one other friend.

Chris : English-Speaking Office Worker

Leah : Korean Office Worker

Chris: How's it going today?

Leah: I'm fine. How are you today?

Chris: Did you catch the game yesterday?

Leah: I did. The athletes played very well. I noticed you are wearing the home team's jersey. Are you a fan?

Chris: Of course, I am. I grew up there.

Leah: How interesting! Do you go to many games?

Chris: I try to make it to as many games as possible, but it gets difficult with the old ball-and-chain.

Leah: Pardon me?

Chris: The old ball-and-chain is a humorous term we use for our significant others. It's like being married is being in jail. How about yours?

Leah: Hmm, I'm not very comfortable talking about my relationships in the office.

Chris: That's understandable. I should be getting back to work. Let's talk more about the game later at lunch!

Leah: Of course. Have a great day.

LET'S DISCUSS

Speak with other students about acceptable dress and conversation topics.

1. How should you dress at the office?

a. How should men dress? Women?

b. Would you rather work in a formal or a casual office? Why?

c. What are ways you could test to see if clothes are acceptable?

2. How are western and eastern styles of dressing different? The same?

a. Do you take your shoes off when you go home? To the office?

b. Do you chew gum in the office? Why?

c. Do you drink beverages such as soda pop or coffee in the office?

3. What are acceptable small talk conversations in Korean offices?

a. How are they different from Western offices?

b. Would you make jokes about the opposite sex in a Korean office? Why?

c. Would you ever make a sexual request in an office? Why?

4. How do you dress differently for Korean holidays?

a. How would you explain the reason you dressed this way?

b. Do you think your form of dress could be a problem?

c. What are Western holidays that you can think of when Westerners dress differently?

5. What are things that offend you? Why?

a. Why should you keep the offensive talk out of the office?

b. What would you do if you heard a popular co-worker make a rude joke or comment?

c. How can crude talk become a problem in an office?

MORE DISCUSSION

Discuss with a partner which of these topics are acceptable to discuss in the office. Why or why not would you include them?

A new product you plan to launch	
A joke about taxi drivers	
A televised sporting event	
A racy scene from a drama	
Your secretary's hair	
A joke about a farmer's daughter	
Your secretary's skirt	
Your family	

SOME THINGS TO REMEMBER

Keeping a Spare

If you commute to work using mass transportation, one tip to wear your nice shoes clean and your feet comfortable is to wear a pair of sneakers on the train or the bus, then change shoes when you arrive at the office. Western offices generally require you to wear shoes the entire day. Walking around in stocking feet is usually unacceptable, so wear your shoes when you are around other people.

Some businesspeople will keep a spare shirt, tie or even an entire suit in their office or the trunk of their car in case of emergencies or spills. This can be a great help if you experience an accident during the middle of the day or do not make it home at night.

You may also want to keep a mirror, razor and small bottles of toiletries in your office, in case you need to freshen yourself up. But don't spend too much time in the bathroom at work. You should prepare at home before coming into work.

One of the most common pieces of advice is: "Dress for the job you want, not the job you have." This means dress better than your peers. You want to look like your boss's boss, not a subordinate.

Unit 6

Writing in the Office

Constructing e-mails, requests and reports

Unit 6

Writing in the Office

Constructing e-mails, requests and reports

Themes and Topics for This Chapter

Office Writing

Constructing to-the-point reports

Common mistakes

Being clear in your writing

Creating a summary

This Lesson's Vocabulary

Focus	Clearly	Concisely	Memo
Readable	Headline	Precise	Specifics
Jumbled	Sort	To-the-Point	Correspondent
Crammed	Tasked	Inboxes	Emoticons

TOPIC

Writing in the Office

When taking English-language courses, most focus is put into listening, reading and speaking, but the important skill, writing, is often not the focus of most classes. Writing clearly and concisely is very important for any office worker, from a secretary to a CEO. In today's office, e-mail has become the most used form of communication, sometimes even more than face-to-face speaking!

Remember, people are busy in an office! They don't have all day to sort through confusing e-mails. Make their job and your job easier by constructing easy-to-read, to the point e-mails. Almost all types of business writing, such as memos, are less important in today's office. However, writing e-mails in the office has replaced most of the old-style writings. E-mail writing's importance has grown, and continues to grow in the business world. However, here are some important tips to keep your writing understandable, short and readable.

First, the subject line of an e-mail should be your headline – or explain the reason for the e-mail. Instead of using the headline "Meeting," tell the reader precise information about the meeting you are writing about. A better headline would be "Planning Meeting: December 15, 2 p.m. Conference Room." This headline gives the important specifics of the meeting: what it is about, when and where.

Another good rule is to make only one point or set of points per e-mail. In the past, writers crammed all sorts of information into one typed letter. This can cause the message to become jumbled and lost in the confusion of other topics. It is perfectly acceptable to write multiple different messages about various subjects. E-mail is also free, so writing multiple messages does not cost any more than writing a single message. So if you are tasked with informing the staff about changes in business policies, a work party and new work IDs, write three separate e-mails about each topic and then send them to the appropriate inboxes.

While e-mail can be formal, you may want to stray away from using "text message language" in your messages. Emoticons, shortened phrases such as "LOL" and other abbreviations should not be used in an English-speaking office. Before sending your e-mail, check the message to make sure it is concise and clear. If you can't find the topic of the message, how can you expect your recipient to discover it? While spell check and grammar check can help, they do not capture all of the mistakes. Take your time as you write your message and then look it over after you finish.

Finally, be a good correspondent. When someone e-mails you, be sure to reply in a timely fashion. Nobody likes waiting for important information!

READING COMPREHENSION

1. Review this list of vocabulary words and then translate the words into Korean.

ENGLISH	KOREAN	ENGLISH	KOREAN
Focus		Concisely	
Readable		Precise	
Jumbled		To-The-Point	
Crammed		Inboxes	
Clearly		Memo	
Headline		Specifics	
Sort		Correspondent	
Tasked		Emoticons	

2. Match the following synonyms with vocabulary words from Question 1.

a. Organize ____________________

b. Short ____________________

c. Exact ____________________

d. Mixed up ____________________

e. Title ____________________

3. Read the statements. Can you tell if they are true or false?

a. E-mailing replaced much other writing in offices. T/F

b. You should never speak face-to-face with somebody. T/F

c. Since e-mail is free, you should send as many as possible. T/F

d. The subject line of an e-mail is not necessary to fill in. T/F

e. Writing is often not the focus of English-language classes. T/F

f. You should never use emoticons in a work e-mail. T/F

g. An e-mail should only have one point or topic. T/F

h. Spell check and grammar check catch every mistake. T/F

WORK WRITING

Now it's time to write freely about using e-mail in the office. Be creative and write for ten minutes.

ROLE PLAY

Practice this conversation with at least one other friend.

Tom : Report Writer

Diana : Report Reader

Tom: Hello, did you get the e-mail I sent about the new identification cards?

Diana: Yes, I did. You wrote very clearly and concisely.

Tom: I noticed you didn't reply. Do you have any questions?

Diana: Yes, when will we need to have our photos taken for the new cards?

Tom: I believe we will have a photographer come in within the next week or so.

Diana: Do we have a scheduled date yet?

Tom: The photos will be taken on a Friday. Does that work for you?

Diana: Fridays are usually very busy for me. Can we schedule a different time for me?

Tom: I may not remember, could you send me an e-mail to my work account as a reminder, please?

Diana: Certainly. Also, did you hear about the planned work party for the holidays?

Tom: Yes, I received your e-mail about that. I just haven't had time to respond.

Diana: Will you go?

Tom: I think so. I need to check my schedule first.

Diana: We will need a head count for the restaurant.

Tom: When I'm back at my desk, I will send you an e-mail.

Diana: Thank you.

LET'S DISCUSS

Speak with other students about business writing.

1. What types of writing will you do for your job?

a. Are you confident in your writing skills? Why?

b. How can you improve your writing?

c. Why do you think writing is not focused on in English-language classes?

2. Do you send many e-mails?

a. How do you send them?

b. Do you prefer to read e-mails on your smart phone or your computer?

c. Do you think people will replace e-mail with a different technology? What?

3. How do you usually send and receive information? E-mail, text messages or FaceBook?

a. Where do you read your e-mails? How has this changed with smart phones?

b. Who sends you the most e-mails? Do you read them all?

c. How do you sort through your mail? Do you delete old messages right away or save them?

MORE DISCUSSION

Discuss with a partner about the types of e-mails you send and who you send them to.

Jokes	
Stories	
Videos	
Notes	
Photos	
Personal Messages	
Memos	
Love Letters	

SOME THINGS TO REMEMBER

Look at this example of a work e-mail. Can you circle all the things that are wrong? How would you write it differently?

SUBJECT: Meting

Hi, Jin,

I was wondering if you are going to show up to the meeting? LOL. I also was wondering where I could find the vacation foms. I am planning to go to Hawaii with my family this year, but I can't seem to remember where the vacation forms are. Hawaii should be fun. I plan on going to a luau and eating lots of fresh pineapple.

So this meeting, what time is it again? I don't feel like looking through my olde e-mails. ☺

Okay, get back to me whenenenver.

Sincerely,

Bill

What errors did you find in this e-mail? How could the writer fix them?

Unit 7

When Problems Arise

What to do when problems arise with work, workers or working

Unit 7

When Problems Arise

What to do when problems arise with work, workers or working

Themes and Topics for This Chapter

Problem solving

Miscommunications

Stress

Talking it out

This Lesson's Vocabulary

Tension	Misconstrued	Predicament	Staff
Consult	Ongoing	Notify	Instances
Resolve	Differing	Lifestyles	Cool head
Sit-down	Undue	Enact	Conducive

TOPIC

When Problems Arise

Any time you put people from different backgrounds together, there is the unfortunate chance of tensions rising, tempers overflowing or information becoming misconstrued or misunderstood. The best thing to do when problems arise is to take a step back, think about the situation and consult the employee handbook to see how to solve the predicament.

Most companies staff a human resources department in order to deal with all types of problems that pop up in an office. For smaller instances, you may want to attempt to resolve the issue yourself if you can. If the problem seems serious, consult the human resources director or a member of the department immediately. If the situation involves an employee's ongoing bad behavior, take notes on the behavior, the frequency and who is affected. Then notify another worker as soon as possible.

Sometimes, differing opinions, work behaviors or lifestyles will conflict. In these situations, keep a cool head and attempt to work with the person who is the cause of the problems. A simple sit-down used to discuss troubles with another employee can clear the air very quickly and the problem-maker may not even know they are causing undue stress to others to coworkers. Opening up about how these troubles affect everybody around them can show the offending party how disruptive they are being inside the office.

When you are the one creating problems, listen to the complaints with honesty and sincerity. Ask how you can change to make the environment more comfortable to everybody, and do the best to enact these changes. An office is not always the most fun, but you must make an effort to keep the work environment conducive to business. Solving personal problems outside of the office ensures prevention of many mishaps, but going to someone with authority is usually the best decision when dealing attempting to solve problems.

READING COMPREHENSION

1. Review this list of vocabulary words and then translate the words into Korean.

ENGLISH	KOREAN	ENGLISH	KOREAN
Tension		Predicament	
Consult		Notify	
Resolve		Lifestyles	
Sit-down		Enact	
Misconstrued		Staff	
Ongoing		Instances	
Differing		Cool head	
Undue		Conducive	

2. Use five of these words or phrases in sentences.

a. Consult ______________________________

b. Resolve ______________________________

c. Ongoing ______________________________

d. Notify ______________________________

e. Conducive ______________________________

3. Read the statements. Can you tell if they are true or false?

a. The human resources department solves inter-office problems. T/F

b. Every work problem requires somebody to get fired. T/F

c. You should keep a cool head when dealing with office problems. T/F

d. People always know they are causing workplace problems. T/F

e. If you are causing issues in the workplace, you should not listen to other people's opinions. T/F

f. You should not worry about offending others with your speech. T/F

g. Workplace problems can always be solved by talking to somebody directly. T/F

h. You should take notes about the problem. T/F

4. Answer the following questions

a. Write about something people do that you find annoying.

____

b. How have you solved disputes in the past?

____

c. Where do you think most problems happen in an office?

____

WORK WRITING

Now it's time to write about your pet peeve or something that annoys you. Make sure to include your past work experiences or other coworkers that bothered you.

ROLE PLAY

Practice this conversation with at least one other friend.

Simon : Problem Employee

Angela : Model Employee

Simon: Why was I called here today?

Angela: I called you here. The other people in the office and I discussed your yelling in the phone.

Simon: Are you telling me that you listen to my phone conversations?

Angela: No, you are so loud we are forced to hear them.

Simon: I can't help it if I get excited when I talk.

Angela: Yes, you can.

Simon: Why should you care how loud I speak?

Angela: A few of us in the office met together and discussed that we find this very disruptive, and sometimes unprofessional.

Simon: Then what do you want me to do about it? Never speak on the phone?

Angela: No, what we want you to do is to speak more quietly on the phone.

Simon: Is there anything else you'd like me to do?

Angela: Refraining from yelling will help everybody in the office remain calm.

LET'S DISCUSS

Speak with other students about problems in the office.

1. What are some common problems you can think of in the office?

a. How can you solve those problems?

b. Have you ever been approached by fellow employees who had a problem with you? What was it?

c. Who can you turn to for help with these problems?

2. Who is usually the problem: men or women?

a. Is there a time of year that brings out troubles in some people? What are they?

b. Where do you think most people have problems in the office? The lunch room? Bathrooms? All around the office?

c. How would you confront a superior who is causing troubles for you? An inferior?

3. What type of cultural differences could cause troubles in the office?

a. What is the best way to deal with a rude co-worker?

b. If a co-worker brought up something embarrassing you did during off hours, how would you deal with the situation?

c. Who should enforce the office area rules?

4. If somebody is stealing other people's lunches from the breakroom, how would you solve this problem?

a. How would you catch this person? Would you try to catch them?

b. Would you ask for this person to be punished? How?

c. How could the situation be prevented?

5. Another employee constantly swears or beats on the computer, how would you deal with this?

a. How about an employee who stays in the bathroom too long?

b. How about an employee that carries on personal phone conversations during work hours?

c. How about an employee that is rude to delivery people?

MORE DISCUSSION

Discuss with a partner how you could solve each of these common workplace problems.

Eating other people's lunches	
Crude comments	
Sleeping at work	
Speaking too loudly	
Stealing office supplies	
Making personal calls during office hours	

SOME THINGS TO REMEMBER

Pranks in the Office

While frowned up, sometimes office pranks can go a long way to embarrass your office problem maker, as well as blow off some steam for you. Light-hearted office pranks have grown in popularity over the years, and some of the pranks you watch on television programs have been repeated and perfected. However, office pranks can and often do go awry. So here are some tips to keep pranks funny as well as safe.

Don't try to humiliate somebody. Pranks should not be painful or life-ruining. Most often they should just poke a little fun at someone. So if you want to fill the office yeller's desk full of ping pong balls, go for it. But don't cause crossfire. You're trying to prank only one of your coworkers, not your entire office. Remember that if you think it's a good idea to stash something smelly in your target's desk, chair or private office. You don't want the entire office to smell bad. Also find out if there are any allergies that might make the office prank a lot less funny.

Test your prank first. If you do a little experiment to see if the prank works, you can fine-tune the joke in order for maximum laughs and minimum effort. Clean up. Pranks don't have to be messy, but sometimes they can become that way. Perhaps the two of you wiping down walls, vacuuming or tidying up the place can be seen as a peaceful olive branch. Of course, make sure the prank is appropriate for your office. You don't want to get fired or reprimanded over a prank!

Unit 8

Time Is Money

When to show up, leave, take lunch and work harder

Unit 8

Time Is Money

When to show up, leave, take lunch and work harder

Themes and Topics for This Chapter

Arriving on time

When to take breaks

Overtime

Lunchtime

Coming in late

This Lesson's Vocabulary

Start time	Media	Field	Awaiting
Majority	Lunchroom	Sanitary	Options
Smelly	Common areas	Permeate	Stench
Errands	Designated	Overtime	Time-and-a-half

TOPIC

When to show up, when to leave, when to stay late

A big difference between Western and Korean offices is the hours workers keep. For most businesses, you will work from 9 a.m. to 5 p.m., with an hour break at noon for lunch. Some places may ask you to come in earlier, or leave later. It all depends on the business. Consult your company handbook, human resources director, manager or a fellow employee about proper times to show up, leave, take breaks and go to lunch.

You may be expected to show up before your start time. Usually, showing up five or ten minutes before or after your start time is acceptable. Some people choose to arrive at the office much earlier so they can read the morning's media concerning their field, drink a cup of coffee, fix makeup, plan the day or respond to awaiting messages.

A majority of businesses will offer a lunch break around noon, for half an hour to an hour. You may bring your own lunch and keep it in the refrigerator, or go out to eat lunch. In crowded business areas, you may need to eat at your desk in the office or the company lunchroom. People suggest you don't eat foods that are easily spilled onto clothes such as spaghetti, but this is all up to you.

If you leave for lunch, make sure you carry your cellphone, pager or means of communication with you. You don't want to miss an important call. Do not go to lunch too far away from the office, as you may be called back for an important meeting, stuck waiting for food or caught in traffic. Showing up late after lunch is not acceptable. Also, eating at your desk near your computer's keyboard is not considered sanitary in some areas, but you may need to do it if there are not other options. Make sure you clean your area and any utensils you used. If your lunch was exceptionally smelly, throw away from common areas as to not permeate the building with the stench.

Depending on your company and job, you will be given other break times. You can use these for smoking, going to the bathroom or running very quick, short errands. Your building may have designated smoking or break areas you may use. Smoking indoors is almost never done in western offices.

Generally, most businesses ask full-time employees to work 40 hours a week, so eight hours every weekday. Occasionally, you may be asked to stay past your usual time. If you are paid hourly you may earn overtime, which usually means "time-and-a-half," this is when you are paid your usual hourly rate, plus half of your usual hourly rate. So let's say you earn $10 an hour, you may be paid $15 an hour if you earn overtime.

Some companies will not pay over time or do not like paying, so make sure you know and have your overtime pay approved. If you earn a salary instead of an hourly rate, you may not be compensated for your overtime. This may just be considered extra work and may help you earn a promotion or pay increase, but sometimes this is just work you do to keep your job.

When quitting time arrives, do all the usual leaving the office jobs. Turn off and lock your computer if you need to, shut off any lights and lock any doors, windows or drawers in your office. If you punch in or out, be sure to do this and enjoy your time off!

READING COMPREHENSION

1. Review this list of vocabulary words and then translate the words into Korean.

ENGLISH	KOREAN	ENGLISH	KOREAN
Start time		Field	
Majority		Sanitary	
Smelly		Permeate	
Errands		Overtime	
Media		Awaiting	
Lunchroom		Options	
Common areas		Stench	
Designated		Time-and-a-half	

2. Use these five words or phrases in sentences.

a. Majority ______________________

b. Media ______________________

c. Stench ______________________

d. Overtime ______________________

e. Time-and-a-half ______________________

3. Match the following synonyms with vocabulary words from Question 1.

a. Clean ____________

b. Chores ____________

c. Odor ____________

d. Job area ____________

e. Choices ____________

4. Read the statements. Can you tell if they are true or false?

a. Breaks during work hours should only be taken during appointed times. T/F

b. You may eat whatever you like for lunch. T/F

c. Some companies will request that you eat at your desk. T/F

d. Generally, you are given one to two hours for lunch. T/F

e. The farther away you take your lunch, the better. T/F

f. Most Western companies ask you to work only 40 hours a week. T/F

g. All businesses pay time-and-a-half for overtime pay. T/F

h. You may arrive and leave whenever you like. T/F

WORK WRITING

Now it's time to write freely about eating lunch in the office. Be creative and write for ten minutes.

ROLE PLAY

Practice this conversation with at least one other friend.

Stella : Manager

Sean : Worker

Stella: What are you doing for lunch today?

Sean: I brought some leftovers from home.

Stella: Oh yeah, what do you have?

Sean: I have some bibimbop and some waffles.

Stella: Sounds good. I would be pleased if you joined me.

Sean: Usually, I would, but I have so much work to finish today, I need to eat and run.

Stella: How about another time?

Sean: My schedule is much more open tomorrow or the next day. Does that work for you?

Stella: Certainly. I want to socialize more with the group and would like to get to know each of my employees better.

Sean: Perhaps we could run out and have a quick cigarette break together today.

Stella: I don't smoke, but I would be happy to join you as you smoke.

Sean: Okay. How does 3 p.m. sound?

Stella: That works for me. I still won't have much time, but I would like to get to know you better as well.

Sean: I will see you at the smoking lounge at 3 p.m.

LET'S DISCUSS

Speak with other students about start, finish, lunch and break times.

1. What do you usually do for lunch?

a. Where will you go for lunch in an office?

b. How much time do you take for lunch?

c. How will this change when you work in an office?

2. If you currently have a job, how long are your hours?

a. How long are your breaks?

b. What do you do during your breaks?

c. What time do you start? Finish?

3. Do you smoke? Where will you take your smoking breaks?

a. Do you get a lunch break or smoking breaks? If so, how long?

b. How are breaks in Western offices different than in Korean offices?

c. If you don't smoke, what will you do during your breaks?

4. How much overtime are you willing to work?

a. Do you think "time-and-a-half" pay is worth it? Why or why not?

b. What types of projects could you expect to cause you to work overtime?

c. How can too much overtime be a burden?

5. How do you wake up in the morning?

a. How can you ensure that you show up at the office on time?

b. What do you do in the morning to get your 'day started?' Do you drink coffee? Exercise? Yoga?

c. What newspapers or websites do you read to stay up-to-date?

SOME THINGS TO REMEMBER

Eat Lunch Like a Pro

Sometimes eating lunch can interfere with your day. Try these tips to avoid problems associated with lunch breaks.

1. Go an hour later or earlier. You can beat long lunch lines, and be at the office during the break when everybody else is out eating.

2. Schedule your lunch. If you mark lunch in your day planner, you always know you need the time for it. Plus, if you cross off things on your to-do list, you can consider eating lunch at the right time an accomplishment.

3. Eat lunch at the same time. This keeps your body in a rhythm, but also lets everyone in your office know where you will be.

4. Keep work at work. Ditch your phone and computer for a nice, quiet and uninterrupted lunch. Read a book or a magazine, play a game on your phone or just relax and enjoy your food! You also might want to eat somewhere else besides your work station.

5. Pack your own lunch. This can help you save money, time and brainpower by removing another choice from your already busy day. If you already know what you're going to eat, you have nothing else to worry about!

6. Eat lunch with friends, and let everybody take turns choosing when and where you go. This keeps some variety in your eating habits, and also eliminates more guessing and choosing.

Unit 9

People in Their Underwear

Holding your own presentations or meetings

OFFICE TALK

Working in an English-Speaking Office

Unit 9

People in Their Underwear

Holding your own presentations or meetings

Themes and Topics for This Chapter

Giving Presentations

Visual Aids

Defeating Anxiety

Body Language

This Lesson's Vocabulary

Diagram	Brainstorm	Visuals	Quotes
Font	Rule of thumb	Uncomfortable	Slideshow
Pertinent	Cap	Rush	Spouse
Note cards	Tone	Gestures	Utilize

TOPIC

Giving a Presentation

If you are doing a great job, you may be asked to give a presentation. Public speaking ranks as one of the most terrifying experiences for some people, but with a little practice and a little work, you can become a great public speaker. The first thing you should do is know your topic. Draw a diagram about your topic, and connect as many words as possible to your topic as you think up. As you brainstorm, think of interesting visuals, quotes, stories or videos that could help your presentation.

There are many rules of thumb about giving a presentation, but sometimes the easiest to remember are the best to use. The KISS Rule is one guidline: Keep It Simple, Stupid. This just means, don't make the presentation any more difficult than it has to be. If you are uncomfortable using PowerPoint or another similar type of technology, don't use it! However, if your presentation requires you to use PowerPoint, keep this formula from Guy Kawasaki in mind: *the 10-20-30 Rule* – Kawasaki says that a presentation should not display more than 10 slides, last longer than 20 minutes or have text smaller than 30 point font. Basically, don't last too long. But what if you have a lot of information to deliver? You don't have to give all of your info, just the most important pieces. Imagine you were on the phone with a friend, but your battery was running out. What would you tell your friend in order to give them all the necessary information? The information you choose is the most important.

Now it is up to you to pick the 10 most important slides. Also remember, slideshows aren't always boring. Apple President Steve Jobs and former United States Vice President Al Gore both made world famous presentations using simple slideshows. You can watch their speeches on YouTube to learn how you can use things from their speeches to make your own speech better. After picking your slides, say a little bit about each one. Sometimes we say a picture is worth 1,000 words, so maybe you can let the slides do the talking. You can point to the pertinent information and then move on to the next image. People in the office are busy, and the shorter your presentation is, sometimes the better it can be. A cap at 20 minutes for your presentation length is perfect, but it doesn't have to fill up the entire time. This isn't to say you need to rush the work you put into your presentation or slideshow. You should practice at least two times. One time you can practice alone, in front of the mirror, a pet or a video recorder. Sometimes it helps just to hear yourself saying the words out loud. The next time you should practice in front of a friend, spouse or family member. Ask them how you did, if they were bored, what they learned, what they liked, didn't like and how you can make it better.

The last part of the 10-20-30 Rule is to use 30-point font. The bigger your words, the more they will stand out. Even if you don't write everything down on your slides, you can still write your speaking points onto note cards and refer to them as you go through your presentation.

Great public speakers show their personality when they speak. They show their sense of humor, use body language and gestures, walk around, make eye contact and adjust tone of their voices to make sure their important points are heard. If you utilize these tips you too can become a great speaker!

READING COMPREHENSION

1. Review this list of vocabulary words and then translate the words into Korean.

ENGLISH	KOREAN	ENGLISH	KOREAN
Diagram		Visuals	
Font		Uncomfortable	
Pertinent		Rush	
Note cards		Gestures	
Brainstorm		Quotes	
Rule of thumb		Slideshow	
Cap		Spouse	
Tone		Utilize	

2. Use five of these words or phrases in sentences.

a. Pertinent ______________________________

b. Brainstorm ______________________________

c. Rush ______________________________

d. Spouse ______________________________

e. Utilize ______________________________

3. Read the statements. Can you tell if they are true or false?

a. You should speak as quickly as possible during a presentation. T/F

b. You can practice in front of the mirror if you want. T/F

c. Presentations can be as long as you want. T/F

d. Good speakers do not need to make eye contact. T/F

e. A speaker should not be entertaining. T/F

f. Many people are afraid of public speaking. T/F

g. You should not have pictures in your presentation. T/F

h. You should make as much eye contact as much as possible. T/F

WORK WRITING

Have you ever given a presentation? What was it about? Who did you give it to? How did it turn out? Do you feel like it was a success? Write a few sentences about things you like to discuss.

ROLE PLAY

Practice this conversation with at least one other friend.

Alan : Speaker

Pearl : Friend

Alan: What are you doing tonight?

Pearl: Nothing special. Why?

Alan: I have to give a presentation at work tomorrow and I was wondering if you had the time to listen to it.

Pearl: Of course. I'd be happy to help.

Alan: Great. I'm incredibly nervous when I speak in front of people.

Pearl: I think everybody is. The trick is to try to relax and imagine people in the underwear.

Alan: Why do people always say that?

Pearl: It's to get you to feel less nervous.

Alan: Does it work?

Pearl: It works for me.

Alan: Any other tips for a newbie public speaker like me?

Pearl: Yeah. Practice, practice, practice makes perfect!

LET'S DISCUSS

Speak with other students about giving presentations.

1. Have you ever given a speech or presentation?

a. What was it about? Who did you give it to?

b. How did you do? How could you improve?

c. Would you do it again? Why?

2. Why are people so nervous with giving presentations?

a. What are ways to become less scared?

b. What do you think the most helpful hint in today's lesson was?

c. How can you build confidence in your speech?

3. Who would you practice your speech with?

a. Why did you choose them?

b. Where would you practice?

c. How many times will you practice?

4. Which famous speaker do you admire?

a. Why do you admire them?

b. What are skills that you can take from them to make yourself a better presenter?

c. What do you notice about their vocabulary, gestures and hand movements?

5. How can you brainstorm?

a. Where can you find interesting quotes?

b. How can you make your speech more interesting?

c. What makes a great speech? A bad speech?

MORE DISCUSSION

Discuss with a partner. What types of presentations could you make about these topics?

Galaxy Tab vs. iPad	
Korea's Government	
Why We Should Plant More Trees	
Explaining Chusok to Foreigners	
How To Sing at Noraebang	
Mistakes While Driving a Car	
Eulji's Best Teachers	
Harry Potter vs. Twilight	

SOME THINGS TO REMEMBER

More Tips for Successful Speaking

1. Try to make eye contact with everybody in the room for a few seconds. When you look at somebody in the eyes, it makes them feel like you are speaking to them personally.

2. Slow your speaking down. No matter how quickly you are used to talking, slow down. You don't want to sound nervous or inexperienced!

3. Summarize your idea and repeat it throughout your presentation to ensure people will remember it!

4. Practice makes permanent! Your practice is only as good as you make it out to be. If you don't practice very hard, you are teaching yourself bad habits. Make your practice matter!

Unit 10

Did You Catch the Show Last Night?

Small Talk with your coworkers

OFFICE TALK

Working in an English-Speaking Office

Unit 10

Did You Catch the Show Last Night?

Small Talk with your coworkers

Themes and Topics for This Chapter

Taboos

Acceptable Topics

Asking For Personal Information

Current Events

This Lesson's Vocabulary

Chatting	Blabbing	Boils down to	Camaraderie
Taboo	Impolite	Socially unacceptable	Plotline
Marital	Attractiveness	Permission	Kindly
Current events	Goings on	Upcoming	Slacking off

TOPIC

Making Small Talk

Americans call it chatting, blabbing or water cooler conversations, but it all boils down to small talk. Small talk is a great way to get to know your fellow employees, the city, culture or your company. It can make you feel like a bigger part of the team, make friends and give you a place in conversations. Of course, your business doesn't pay you to talk, so you don't want to make small talk a big part of your day, but it helps to build camaraderie in the office.

Small talk can generally be about anything, but you want to avoid talking about taboo subjects. What's a taboo? A taboo is anything somebody feels uncomfortable talking about, impolite or is something socially unacceptable to discuss in many conversations. Some differences between Korean and Western cultures is that Westerners may not want to discuss their age, weight, marital status, religion, politics as well as how much they paid for a car, gift, house or other item.

If you are curious about a taboo topic, you can just ask, "Is it okay if I ask about..." This shows you are requesting permission to find out more personal information. If you are really interested in learning more about your co-workers' personal lives, you can begin your question with "Is it okay/alright/cool if I ask you if you are: married/have kids/how much you paid for your car?" If the person wants to answer, they will. If they don't, they should kindly say "No. That's personal."

You should also refrain from speaking poorly, such as insulting, about other people in your company. This is a common office topic, but you don't want to be seen as somebody who talks about somebody behind their back. We call those people "gossips" and they are generally not respected. Also, if you insult somebody who isn't there, people will assume you say the same type of things about them when they are not present.

For the most part, small talk is about "small" subjects that most people find interesting:

sports, television programs, current events or goings on around the office. So you may find yourself chatting about topics you might not care about, but you may continue anyway just to keep the conversations going. Around special events or holidays people may small talk more than usual, which can lighten the mood of the office. People want to discuss results of a game, the weather, any plans for an upcoming holiday, a plotline to drama or any number of things.

You want to remember, a little small talk is okay, but too much can make it seem like you are slacking off, which is definitely not what you want to be doing. It's up to you to find the fine line between a polite conversationalist and the office bore.

READING COMPREHENSION

1. Review this list of vocabulary words and then translate the words into Korean.

ENGLISH	KOREAN	ENGLISH	KOREAN
Chatting		Boils Down To	
Taboo		Socially Unacceptable	
Goings On		Permission	
Current Events		Upcoming	
Blabbing		Camaraderie	
Impolite		Kindly	
Attractiveness		Slacking Off	

2. Match the following synonyms with vocabulary words from Question 1.

a. Rude ____________________

b. Good Looks ____________________

c. Nicely ____________________

d. Forbidden ____________________

e. Friendship ____________________

3. Read the statements. Can you tell if they are true or false?

a. Westerners do not like to discuss their age or weight. T/F

b. Small talk can build friendships. T/F

c. You can ask permission to talk about something taboo. T/F

d. A person doesn't need to answer a taboo question. T/F

e. Talking about money can be taboo. T/F

f. Some people view chatting as slacking off. T/F

g. You should small talk as much as possible. T/F

WORK WRITING

What do you like to talk about with your friends? Your co-workers? Strangers? Write a few sentences about things you like to discuss.

ROLE PLAY

Practice this conversation with at least one other friend.

Eusang: Korean Worker

Irene: Western Worker

Eusang: Hi. I really like your car. I'd like one similar to it. I'm curious. Can I ask how much you paid for your car?

Irene: My car? Well, I suppose it's okay to discuss between friends and co-workers. I paid about $30,000 for my car. I have always wanted one like this.

Eusang: Oh, thank you very much. Are you still enjoying it?

Irene: It drives well and my family likes it.

Eusang: Is it okay to ask, how long have you been married?

Irene: I've been married to my spouse for about five years now. How about yourself, can I ask if you're married?

Eusang: I'm not married as of now, but I'm hoping to soon.

Irene: I'm sure you'll find the right person any time now. Hey, I was watching a TV program last night and I'm wondering if you saw it. Do you watch "American Idol?"

Eusang: I do. In my country it's called "Super Star K."

Irene: Oh wow, it's in Korea too?

Eusang: It's very popular. Didn't the show originate in England?

LET'S DISCUSS

Speak with other students about small talk and taboo topics.

1. What are ways you can ask permission to talk about something taboo?

a. Should you talk about something taboo? Why?

b. What are topics you find taboo?

c. What are some differences between Western and Korean beliefs about taboo?

2. What are some small talk topics you enjoy?

a. What are small talk topics that bore you?

b. What is more interesting, the weather or a television program?

c. Do you like sports? TV Dramas? Holidays?

3. How long should you small talk at work?

a. What are some problems that can arise from small talk?

b. How can small talk help build friendships?

c. Why should you be friendly with your co-workers?

4. What is going on right now that interests you?

a. What's a current event that fascinates you?

b. Is there a drama, movie, song, sport or other piece of art you are interested in? Why?

5. What would you do if a co-worker brought up a topic you were uncomfortable talking about?

a. How can you politely exit the conversation?

b. Would you tell a superior member of the office? Why?

c. If you were a manager, how could you limit the small talk at work?

MORE DICUSSION

Discuss with a partner, what types of conversations could you have about these topics?

Christmas	
Chusok	
Super Star K	
Baseball	
The Superbowl	
A Boring Meeting	
Your Favorite Celebrity	
The Weather	

SOME THINGS TO REMEMBER

Making More Small Talk Everywhere

Small talk can make you seem like a more open and friendly person but small talk should not be stressful. However, striking up conversations with other people you don't know can be nerve wracking, so small talk can be a challenge for some people. Here are some tips to help you improve your confidence when starting small talks:

1. Talk with everybody you meet, everywhere you go. You can talk with co-workers, friends of friends, waiters, cashiers, other passengers on the bus and people waiting in lines.

2. Keep up to date. Read the news, magazines, blogs or other things you might think people will find interesting. You never know what people might like!

3. Start conversations. If there are people around, you can make some small talk. So try and chat with people at parties, waiting rooms or the bus. Usually chatting about the weather or something somebody is reading is a great start.

4. Don't take offense. If somebody doesn't want to talk, it probably has nothing to do with you. Everybody has good and bad days. Maybe you met them on a bad day. Don't let their bad day ruin yours.

Unit 11

First Shot, Last Call

Socializing with work friends out of work

Unit 11

First Shot, Last Call

Socializing with work friends out of work

Themes and Topics for This Chapter

Hanging out with coworkers

Afterhours

Overdrinking

This Lesson's Vocabulary

Blow off some steam	Social lubricant	Afterhours	Merry
Immediate	Stumbling drunk	Drinking games	Dissimilarity
Hierarchy	Being verbally abusive	Intoxication	Haunt
On the clock	Reprimanded	Terminated	Know when to say when

TOPIC

Afterhours

Just as small talk can help build friendships and pass the time during shifts, socializing with your coworkers is another way to blow off some steam and relax. Some offices will have work functions or social clubs to assist in afterhours time, but sometimes the workers will just gather at a bar, restaurant or other meeting place to eat, drink and be merry.

One immediate difference between drinking in Korea and drinking in the Western world is that generally, when with coworkers Westerners do not like to drink until they are stumbling drunk. For the most part, social events organized by your office or coworkers are to gather for a meal or perhaps a few drinks. Most likely, you will not be playing drinking games or singing songs. This may sound a little more boring than drinking in Korea, but you can make other friends to hang out with besides the people who work with you.

Another dissimilarity is that there usually is not the strict social hierarchy in Western offices. Everybody is allowed to hang out with everybody. Your superior office workers will not force you to take shots as sometimes happens in Korea.

Finally, the last big difference is that what you do outside of the office, whether it be drinking too much, being verbally abusive or making unwanted sexual advances to a coworker, this can come back to haunt you in the office. Even though you are technically not on the clock, you can still be reprimanded or even terminated for your actions after quitting time.

So instead of drinking to the point of intoxication, relax on the alcohol and "know when to say when," which is a famous saying about stopping drinking when you have drunk too much. On some occasions, you may find yourself or others imbibing too much, but do your best to avoid it. These are people you work with, and you do not want to put yourself, or somebody else in a situation when one of you can get in trouble.

Do your best not to show up hungover, which is self-explanatory. Also, as you talk with friends during an outing, just like with small talk, you should avoid berating a colleague who is not present. If others are doing it, that may be alright, but for the most part, it just shows poor manners.

Last of all, under no circumstances should you drink alcohol and then drive. Driving under the influence of alcohol (DUI) is a serious offense in the Western world, especially in the United States. A DUI will cost you large fines, make your car insurance become more expensive and may even cause you to serve some jail time. You can take a cab if you have had too much, find a designated driver or you can refrain from having drinks.

READING COMPREHENSION

1. Review this list of vocabulary words and then translate the words into Korean.

ENGLISH	KOREAN	ENGLISH	KOREAN
Blow off some steam		Afterhours	
Immediate		Drinking games	
Hierarchy		Intoxication	
On the clock		Terminated	
Social lubricant		Merry	
Stumbling drunk		Dissimilarity	
Being verbally abusive		Haunt	
Reprimanded		Know when to say when	

2. Use five of these words or phrases in sentences.

a. Blow off some steam ______________________

b. Hierarchy ______________________

c. Terminated ______________________

d. Merry ______________________

e. Dissimilarity ______________________

3. Match the following synonyms with vocabulary words from Question 1.

a. Intoxicated ______________

b. Fired ______________

c. Disturb ______________

d. Insulting ______________

e. Relax ______________

4. Read the statements. Can you tell if they are true or false?

a. You should drink as much as possible during a work outing. T/F

b. You should not talk poorly about people when they are not present. T/F

c. Your actions outside of work have consequences. T/F

d. Drinking and driving is a serious crime in the United States. T/F

e. Westerners don't like drinking games. T/F

f. Western offices follow a strict hierarchy. T/F

g. During an office party, you should tell your boss how much you don't like working at your office. T/F

h. You can take the bus if you do not want to drive while drunk. T/F

WORK WRITING

Now it's time to write freely about afterhours work events. Be creative and write for ten minutes

ROLE PLAY

Practice this conversation with at least one other friend.

Alvin : Worker 1

Rachael : Worker 2

Alvin: Wow, it's great to finally hang out with you after work.

Rachael: Yeah. I have wanted to get to know some of my fellow employees a little bit better.

Alvin: Me, too. We don't get enough time to hang out.

Rachael: Do you usually come to this bar?

Alvin: Sometimes. I really like their happy hour.

Rachael: Oh, cool. I usually go to a place near my house for drinks.

Alvin: Okay. So would you like to do some shots?

Rachael: I'm not feeling well enough to do shots and I also have to drive. I was hoping to just have a quiet drink or two.

Alvin: No pressure. Do you think the mail room staff is a little weird? Every time I need to send or receive a package, I find them doing something odd.

Rachael: I don't know if I feel comfortable talking about somebody who is not here.

Alvin: I suppose you're right.

Rachael: So are you working on anything interesting now?

LET'S DISCUSS

Speak with other students about socializing with coworkers after work.

1. How often do you like to drink a week? A month?

a. What do you usually drink?

b. How much do you usually drink?

c. Would you want to drink that much around a coworker? Why or why not?

2. Why do you think Westerners don't like to drink that much around coworkers?

a. What are some other drinking habit differences between Koreans and Westerners?

b. How much money do you spend on alcohol when you go out?

c. Do you prefer bars, clubs, restaurants or parties? Why?

3. Why do you think drinking and driving laws are so strict in the Western world?

a. What are some ways to avoid drinking and driving?

b. How can you test yourself to see if you are too drunk to drive?

c. When is it time to stop drinking?

4. What would you talk about during a work outing?

a. What would you do if the conversation moved to talking poorly about a coworker?

b. Why would you not want to bad mouth a coworker?

c. Besides drinking alcohol, what could you do?

5. What are some differences between Western and Korean drinking cultures?

a. What kinds of food do you like?

b. Where do you go?

c. When do you socialize with your coworkers?

SOME THINGS TO REMEMBER

Drinking and Driving Facts

Before you get behind the wheel while intoxicated, think about these facts.

1. Drunk driving causes approximately one-third of all traffic fatalities in the United States.
2. On average, someone in the U.S. is killed by a drunk driver every 40 minutes.
3. According to the law in all 50 U.S. states, a driver is considered to be legally drunk when his or her blood alcohol content (BAC) level is at or above .08 grams per deciliter (g/dL).[e]
4. To reach a BAC level of .08 g/dL, a man weighing approximately 65 kilograms would need to consume four standard drinks in one hour on an empty stomach. A woman weighing about 63.5 kilograms would need to consume three drinks in one hour.
5. It takes approximately six hours after drinking for the body to completely eliminate alcohol from its system.
6. A driver with a BAC of .08 g/dL is 11 times more likely to be in a fatal accident than a driver who has consumed no alcohol.
7. The highest rates of drunk driving occur among drivers aged 21-24. This age group makes up 35% of alcohol-impaired drivers involved in fatal collisions.
8. Motorcycle drivers are the most likely to be involved in fatal drunk driving accidents, with 27% of such accidents in 2007 involving at least one drunk motorcycle operator.
9. Nearly 75% of drunk drivers involved in fatal collisions are not wearing their safety belts.
10. State laws commonly use two different acronyms to describe drunken or impaired driving—DWI and DUI. DWI stands for "driving while intoxicated" and typically refers only to alcohol impairment, while DUI stands for "driving under the influence" and can refer to either alcohol or drugs.
11. Beer is the most common type of alcoholic beverage involved in both DUI arrests and fatal crashes, according to the National Highway Traffic Safety Administration (NHSTA). It is also the drink of choice in most cases of binge drinking and underage drinking.
12. To determine if a driver is legally impaired, a police officer will typically administer breathalyzer test. A breathalyzer is a machine that estimates a driver's blood alcohol content level by determining the amount of alcohol in his or her lungs.

Unit 12

Can I Take a Message?

Using the telephone at the office

Unit 12

Can I Take a Message?

Using the telephone at the office

Themes and Topics for This Chapter

Using the Phone

Taking Messages

Making a Talking Plan

This Lesson's Vocabulary

Face-to-face	Interactions	Style	Improve
Refresher	Distracted	Constructing	On hold
Cheat sheet	On point	On the line	Right away
Access information	Handy	Objective	Social time

TOPIC

On the Line

Along with good face-to-face interactions, employers and customers want to experience good telephone interactions. Your "telephone voice" or "telephone style" can be very important and this chapter will look at ways to help you improve the time you are on the phone.

As a refresher, you should answer every call at work with "Hello, (your name and your title) how can I help you?" Beside your phone, you should also keep a pen and a pad of paper to write notes or messages. Another helpful addition is to tape your business card or sheet with all your contact information, or contact info you use often on your computer screen or wall. At the end of your conversation, if they called you say, "Thank you for calling and have a great day." If you called them, "Thank you for speaking with me today. Have a great day."

Talking on the telephone adds some difficulties because you cannot see the other person and what they are doing. Often, people become distracted while they are on the phone. They may try to check e-mail, organize their desk or any number of office activities. However, if you are on the phone, you should have a goal: whether you want to make a sale, find out some information, complain, get off of hold or just get off the phone.

Constructing a "phone talking plan" is a great start. This can be a little "cheat sheet" to help you stay on point while you are on the line. First, figure out who you need to speak with to reach your goal. Is there a specific person or a specific job title you are looking for? Find that out right away, if you can.

Next, this issue deals with time. How long would you like to speak? Five minutes, twenty minutes or longer? Is there a good time to call? How much time are you willing to wait on hold?

After that, what are important phrases or questions you want to ask? If you need a specific number, password, name or other access information, keep that near you and handy. The most crucial part of your talking plan is: What type of information are you looking for? What is your objective of this call? This is business time, not social time, so you should not be calling people just to talk with them and see how their day is going.

Finally, if you do not get through to the person you want to speak with and have to leave a message, what are you going to say? Usually, you would leave your name, where you work, the reason you called, a phone number where you can be reached and a good time to call. On the other side of the phone, if you are taking messages for somebody else, make sure you get all the important information about the call. Who called? Why did they call? When did they call? Where were they calling from? What were they calling about? What is a number, e-mail address or screen name where they can be reached? Some companies will have pre-made message taking sheets available to employees.

READING COMPREHENSION

1. Review this list of vocabulary words and then translate the words into Korean.

ENGLISH	KOREAN	ENGLISH	KOREAN
Face-to-face		Style	
Refresher		Constructing	
Cheat sheet		On the Line	
Access information		Objective	
Interactions		Improve	
Distracted		On hold	
On point		Right away	
Handy		Social time	

2. Match the following synonyms with vocabulary words from Question 1.

a. Immediately ____________________

b. Building ____________________

c. Sidetracked ____________________

d. Useful ____________________

e. In person ____________________

3. Read the statements. Can you tell if they are true or false?

a. You should always give your name, cell phone and salary to a caller. T/F

b. Keeping a business card or information sheet near your phone can keep all your important information right where you need it. T/F

c. You should end phone calls with a "Thank you." T/F

d. People are rarely distracted on the phone. T/F

e. Some people don't like talking on the phone. T/F

f. Having a talking plan or an objective may cost you more time. T/F

g. If the caller does not need to speak with you, you should offer to take a message for them anyway. T/F

h. Business time is social time. T/F

WORK WRITING

Now it's time to write freely about using the phone at work. Be creative and write for ten minutes.

ROLE PLAY

Practice this conversation with at least one other friend.

Charles : Caller

Lisa : Answerer

Lisa: Hello, Lisa Kent, Bugle Planet Marketing Director. How may I help you?

Charles: Hi, Lisa, I'm Charles Murray from W.A.C. Industries. I was wondering if I could get some information about your new gadget.

Lisa: Sure, what would you like to know?

Charles: First off, let me look at my notes and questions, when will it be available to the public?

Lisa: We hope to release our gadget within the next six months.

Charles: And what is the contact information?

Lisa: Do you want an address, a phone number or the e-mail for the person running the project?

Charles: All three if possible.

Lisa: Okay, our address is 44 Market Street New York, NY 11122; to call, it's 555-1234; and if you want to e-mail you can reach me at Kent@Bugleplanet.com.

Charles: I'm sorry. Was that PKent@Bugleplanet.com?

Lisa: No, you don't need the "P" in front of my name.

Charles: Thanks. What is a good time to call you for more information?

Lisa: You can reach me any time from 1 p.m. to 5 p.m., but I will be on vacation next week so you can call William Reilly at 555-1235.

Charles: And can I speak to him today?

Lisa: Unfortunately, he is out at the moment. Can I take a message?

Charles: Yes.

Lisa: Can I get your name, a phone number and what you would like to ask him?

LET'S DISCUSS

Speak with other students about using the phone at work.

1. How much time do you spend on the phone?

a. Why do you usually talk on the phone?

b. How often do you speak for business?

c. How are Korean phone manners different than Western?

2. Do you make a telephone plan? Why or why not?

a. How do you find the information you need?

b. How long are you willing to wait on hold?

c. What information will you give you need to leave a message?

3. What are some rude things to do on the phone?

a. Is it more important to be nice or to be efficient? Why?

b. How do you answer telemarketers?

c. Do you prefer to talk on the phone or send and receive e-mail?

4. What is your last great experience with a business call?

a. How did that call change your perception of the company?

b. What is your last bad experience with a business call?

c. How can you improve your English skills on the phone?

5. By what title do you prefer to be called when somebody phones you?

a. How do you feel when somebody uses the wrong title?

b. Discuss the phrase "Phoning it in."

c. Who do you make most of your phone calls to?

SOME THINGS TO REMEMBER

Useful Everyday Questions on the Phone

Whether you're going to ring your family, friends, boss or stranger, plan out your next telephone call in English – even if you will be speaking Korean.

1. Who am I calling?

2. Best time of day to call?

3. If that person isn't available, who should I ask for?

4. Questions I want to ask.

5. Questions they may ask me.

6. Any access information, passwords, telephone numbers or addresses I may need.

7. Useful English phrases I may need to use.

8. How long am I willing to wait on hold?

9. What will I say if I am going to leave a message?

10. (After the call) Was the call successful? Why or why not?

Unit 13

Moving On

Promotions, quitting, downsizing and terminations

Unit 13

Moving On

Promotions, quitting, downsizing and terminations

Themes and Topics for This Chapter

How to Deal with Losing a Job

Looking for a New Job

When it's Time to Find a New Job

How To Quit

This Lesson's Vocabulary

Promoted	Downsized	Terminated	Part ways
Brag	Reference	Big scene	Good fortune
Phrases	Negatively affecting	Budget	Discard
Cuts	Losing your job	Position	Suited for

TOPIC

Moving On

According to some data, people in the United States change jobs once every 3.5 years. While the accuracy of this information is debatable, chances are, you too will change your job in the future. There are many ways for you to change your job. You may be promoted, quit, downsized (let go) or terminated (fired). Sometimes finding a new job is your choice, sometimes the decision is up to board members you may have never met, and sometimes the time is just right for you and your place of employment to part ways.

No matter how terrible your position is, you want to leave on good terms whenever you move on from a job, whether you're promoted or fired. Who knows when you might need to use some of these people as a reference, have them write letters of recommendation or even work with them again?

While making a big scene in the office like they do on the movies may seem like a great idea, remember, those are just movies. The business world can be very small, so you do not want to be embarrassed every time you run into these people, or for those people to speak with other potential employers.

If you are promoted, congratulations! You are moving up in the company, and the world. The important thing to remember is not to brag about your promotion. Even if you put a lot of hard work, effort and time into earning this promotion, you do not want to insult others by boasting about your good fortune. You may tell others, but avoid using phrases like, "I'm the best!" or "I thought it would never happen!"

How can you know if you should quit your job? You need to ask yourself many questions. Do you enjoy anything about your work? Do you find anything challenging? Are you proud of what you do? Do you believe in your work? Could you find a better job elsewhere? Are you uncomfortable or are people not listening to you at work? Is your job negatively affecting your life? Do you need the money bad enough to keep a job you do not like?

If you feel that the time has come that you need to quit your job, most people suggest telling your manager at least two weeks in advance, but you may request even more time. The company will need to replace you and that may take some time. You will still need to show up at the office, but that doesn't have to be a bad thing. During your two-week period make notes about what you liked and didn't like about the company and make sure you finish up any projects you were working on at the old job.

People are downsized when the company no longer has room or the budget to keep them. Downsizing has become an increasingly popular way for companies around the world to discard unneeded employees. The important thing to remember when you are downsized is that you personally did not do anything wrong. The company may be reorganizing or going through some budget cuts. While nobody likes to feel unwanted, being downsized is unfortunately one of the most rapidly rising reasons people are leaving positions. Most companies will end up hiring more workers when times improve.

The last way people switch jobs is what is commonly called as "getting fired." Getting fired means your boss no longer wishes you to show up for work. This may be because of something you did, said, have been doing or have been saying. This can be the most painful way to lose your job, because you know it is your fault that you are losing your job. The important thing to remember is that you can always find a new job. It may not be the ideal job, but perhaps with a little luck and some more hard work, you can move into a position better suited for you.

READING COMPREHENSION

1. Review this list of vocabulary words and then translate the words into Korean.

ENGLISH	KOREAN	ENGLISH	KOREAN
Promoted		Terminated	
Brag		Big scene	
Phrases		Budget	
Cuts		Position	
Downsized		Part ways	
Reference		Good fortune	
Negatively affecting		Discard	
Losing your job		Suited for	

2. Use the five words or phrases in sentences.

a. Brag ______________________________

b. Budget ______________________________

c. Reference ______________________________

d. Losing Your Job ______________________________

e. Big Scene ______________________________

3. Answer the following questions.

a. Write about how you would quit your current job.

____

b. What can you do to cheer yourself up if you've been fired?

____

c. How can starting a new job be a good thing?

____

4. Read the statements. Can you tell if they are true or false?

a. Downsizing happens when nobody at your job likes you. T/F

b. Bragging about a promotion is considered poor manners. T/F

c. You should be nice to people at your old company because you might need to speak to them again in the future. T/F

d. Workers are automatically promoted after one year. T/F

e. It is proper to give three weeks' notice when quitting a job. T/F

f. You can be fired from any job for any reason. T/F

g. Budget cuts cause many people to get promotions. T/F

h. Downsizing can be the result of reorganization of the company. T/F

WORK WRITING

Now it's time to write freely about quitting, being terminated, getting laid off or any other way of moving from one job to another. Be creative and write for ten minutes.

ROLE PLAY

Practice this conversation with at least one other friend.

Luke : Worker

Han : Manager

Luke: I called you to this personal meeting so that we may discuss my future.

Han: Alright. What would you like to talk about?

Luke: I have worked at this company for four years now, and I would like end my employment here.

Han: Why is that?

Luke: I have found a better position suited to my talents. This new job pays me more and allows me to be more creative.

Han: Well, congratulations. We'll be sad to lose you, but I'm sure you will do well at the other company.

Luke: Yes, I wish things could have worked out better, but I need to follow up on this.

Han: You need to chase your opportunities when you can.

Luke: Is it possible to use you for a reference in the future?

Han: Of course.

Luke: I was also wondering if I could get a letter of recommendation.

Han: I would be happy to write one. When would you like your last day to be?

Luke: I am hoping to start my new position in two weeks.

Han: Okay. We will schedule your last day two weeks from now. Thank you for talking to us.

LET'S DISCUSS

Speak with other students about moving on to a new job.

1. Have you ever been fired? Downsized? What happened?

a. How did you find out?

b. How did you feel?

c. Who told you?

2. Have you ever quit a job? What happened?

a. Why did you quit?

b. How did you inform the company?

c. How long did you work until your time was finished?

3. Have you ever been downsized? What happened?

a. How long did it take for you to find a new job?

b. Did the company succeed after you left? If so, how? If not, what happened?

c. How did you find out?

4. What do you think are the best reasons for quitting?

a. When should you quit a job?

b. Have you ever fired anybody? What happened?

c. Is the way Koreans quit jobs different than the way Westerners quit jobs?

5. Why should you be nice to the people at your old job?

a. What are things your former fellow employees can do for you after you are finished working there?

b. How can you look for new jobs?

c. What is the meanest firing story you've ever heard?

SOME THINGS TO REMEMBER

What to do After You Lose a Job

Employees are terminated for many reasons. The important thing to remember is that all types of people have been fired or failed at their jobs in one way or another. Abraham Lincoln failed at many things throughout his personal life and career, but ended up being one of the most successful American presidents.

Here are some things that might help you feel better if you are fired.

1. Join a club. Now that you have more free time, you can always try to improve yourself with your hobbies!

2. Go Back to School! You're never too old to learn something new.

3. Keep a Diary. Write notes to yourself about your job, your coworkers, what you liked and disliked about the job. Nobody needs to see these thoughts, but it may be therapeutic to put them on paper.

4. Join a Support Group. You may find support groups for people who have lost their jobs. It may be comforting in hearing other people's stories.

5. Vacation Time. You can take that nice long vacation you've always wanted.

6. Cleaning time. Do a full cleaning on your entire living space, car, luggage and everything else.

7. Start Your Own Business. If you're able, this is a great time to hang out your own shingle and start working for somebody who will never fire you...You!

REFERENCES

Myeong-Hee Seong and Katie Mae Klemsen. (2009). Get Real! Discussion and Debate for English Language Learners. Seoul. Backsan Publishing.

Myeong-Hee Seong and Katie Mae Klemsen. (2010). *You're Hired!. Resume & Letter Writing for English Language Learners*. Seoul. Backsan Publishing.

Myeong-Hee Seong and Katie Mae Klemsen. (2011). Interview English. Seoul. Backsan Publishing.

http://facts.randomhistory.com/2009/08/28_drunk-driving.html

Answer Key

[Unit 1]

2 a. Plan-prepare b. Sway-influence c. Acquire-land
d. Papers-documents e. Conference-interview

3 a. F b. T c. T d. F e. F f. T g. T h. F

[Unit 2]

3 a. F b. F c. T d. T e. F f. T g. T h. F

[Unit 3]

3 a. T b. T c. F d. F e. T f. F g. F h. T

[Unit 4]

3 a. F b. T c. T d. F e. T f. F g. F h. F

[Unit 5]

2 a. Talk-chat b. Manual-handbook c. Easy going-liberal
d. Gaudy-flashy e. Rules-guidelines

3 a. F b. T c. T d. F e. T f. T g. F h. F

[Unit 6]

2 a. Organize-sort b. Short-precise c. Exact-precise
d. Mixed up-jumbled e. Title-Headline

3 a. T b. F c. F d. F e. T f. T g. T h. F

[Unit 7]

2 a. T b. F c. T d. F e. F f. F g. F h. T

[Unit 8]

3 a. Clean-sanitary b. Chores-errands c. Odor-stench
d. Job area-common area e. Choices-options

4 a. T b. T c. T d. F e. F f. T g. F h. F

[Unit 9]

2 a. F b. T c. F d. F e. F f. T g. F h. T

[Unit 10]

2 a. Rude-impolite b. Good Looks-attractiveness c. Nicely-kindly
d. Forbidden-taboo e. Friendship-camaraderie

3 a. T b. T c. T d. T e. T f. T g. F

[Unit 11]

3 a. Intoxicated-stumbling drunk b. Fired-terminated c. Disturb-Haunt
d. Insulting-being verbally abusive e. Relax-blow off some steam

4 a. F b. T c. T d. T e. F f. F g. F h. T

[Unit 12]

2 a. Immediately-right away b. Building-constructing
c. Sidetracked-distracted d. Useful-handy
e. In Person-face-to-face

3 a. F b. T c. T d. F e. T f. F g. T h. F

[Unit 13]

4 a. F b. T c. T d. F e. F f. T g. F h. T

Authors

Myeong-Hee Seong

Ph. D. in English Education, Korea University

Professor, Eulji University

Casey Freeman

M.A. in Journalism, University of Colorado

Professor, Eulji University

Office Talk

2011년 12월 15일 초판 1쇄 인쇄
2011년 12월 20일 초판 1쇄 발행

공저자 Myeong-Hee Seong
Casey Freeman
발행인 (寅製) 진 욱 상

저자와의 합의하에 인지첩부 생략

발행처 백산출판사
서울시 성북구 정릉3동 653-40
등록 : 1974. 1. 9. 제 1-72호
전화 : 914-1621, 917-6240
FAX : 912-4438
http://www.ibaeksan.kr
editbsp@naver.com

값 14,000원
ISBN 978-89-6183-548-0